WHEN I GO TO
GROCERY
STORE

Alan Walker

CRABTREE
PUBLISHING COMPANY
WWW.CRABTREEBOOKS.COM

Our bodies need food.

But where does food come from?

Yes, you can get food from the grocery store.

But before it gets to the store, farmers grow it or **raise** it.

Farmers sell to companies who prepare and package food.

Steps to getting food to the store:

1 Farmers grow or raise the food.

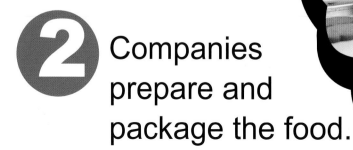

2 Companies prepare and package the food.

3 Trucks deliver the food to stores.

4 We buy the food at the store.

13

So next time you eat,
think of the farmer.

Think of the people who prepare and package the food.

Think of the people who deliver it to the stores.

And think about all the great food choices we have.

Glossary

choices (CHOYSS-iz): Choices are all the things you can choose from.

companies (KUHM-puh-neez): Companies are businesses that make things or provide services. There are companies that make cereal.

prepare (pri-PAIR): To prepare is to take steps to make something, or to be ready for something.

raise (RAYZ): To raise an animal is to feed and take care of it.

Index

School-to-Home Support for Caregivers and Teachers

Crabtree Seedlings books help children grow by letting them practice reading. Here are a few guiding questions to help the reader with building his or her comprehension skills. Possible answers are included.

Before Reading

- What do I think this book is about? I think this book is about going shopping for food at a grocery store.

- What do I want to learn about this topic? I want to learn about where food comes from.

During Reading

- I wonder why... I wonder why food needs to be prepared. What kinds of things do companies do to prepare food?

- What have I learned so far? I have learned that food comes from farms.

After Reading

- What details did I learn about this topic? I learned that there are four steps to getting food. First, farmers grow or raise food. Next, companies prepare and package food. Then, trucks deliver food to grocery stores. Last, we buy food at a grocery store.

- Read the book again and look for the vocabulary words. I see the word **_raise_** on page 8 and the word **_choices_** on page 20. The other vocabulary words are found on pages 22 and 23.

Library and Archives Canada Cataloging-in-Publication Data

Title: When I go to the grocery store / Alan Walker.
Names: Walker, Alan, 1963- author.
Description: Series statement: In my community | "A Crabtree seedlings book". | Includes index.
Identifiers: Canadiana 20200388134 |
  ISBN 9781427129611 (hardcover) |
  ISBN 9781427129710 (softcover)
Subjects: LCSH: Food industry and trade—Juvenile literature. | LCSH: Food—Juvenile literature.
Classification: LCC TP370.3 .W35 2021 | DDC j641.3—dc23

Library of Congress Cataloging-in-Publication Data

Names: Walker, Alan, 1963- author.
Title: When I go to the grocery store / Alan Walker.
Description: New York : Crabtree Publishing, 2021. | Series: In my community : a Crabtree seedlings book | Includes index.
Identifiers: LCCN 2020050798 |
  ISBN 9781427129611 (hardcover) |
  ISBN 9781427129710 (paperback)
Subjects: LCSH: Grocery shopping--Juvenile literature.
Classification: LCC TX356 .W35 2021 | DDC 641.3/1--dc23
LC record available at https://lccn.loc.gov/2020050798

Crabtree Publishing Company

www.crabtreebooks.com   1-800-387-7650
e-book ISBN 978-1-947632-77-6
Print book version produced jointly with Crabtree Publishing Company NY, USA

Written by Alan Walker
Production coordinator and Prepress technician: Ken Wright
Print coordinator: Katherine Berti

Printed in the U.S.A ./012021/CG20201112

Photo credits: istock.com, Shutterstock.com, Pg2; dulezidar, Pg3; istock.com/monkeybusinessimages, Pg.4; istock.com/joey333, Pg.5; istock.com/gopixa, Pg.6/7; istock.com/OceanFishing, Pg.8/9; istock.com/Toltek, Pg.9; istock.com/NikonShutterman, Pg10; istock.com/WEzekial, Pg11; istock.com/Riccardo_Mojana and agnormark, Pg12; istock.com/fotokostic and boggy22, Pg13; istock.com/JackF, Pg14; istock.com/HughStonelan, Pg15; istock.com/jenoche, Pg16; istock.com/jfmdesign, Pg17; istock.com/RossHelen, Pg18; istock.com/ Pg 19; Shutterstock.com/ VGstockstudio, Pg20/21 DragonImages,

Published in Canada	Published in the United States	Published in the United Kingdom	Published in Australia
Crabtree Publishing	Crabtree Publishing	Crabtree Publishing	Crabtree Publishing
616 Welland Ave.	347 Fifth Ave	Maritime House	Unit 3 – 5
St. Catharines, ON	Suite 1402-145	Basin Road North, Hove	Currumbin Court
L2M 5V6	New York, NY 10016	BN41 1WR	Capalaba QLD 4157